crocheted
HOODS & COWLS

crocheted HOODS & COWLS

20 Enchanting Designs *for* Women
7 Adorable Animal Hoods *for* Kids

TAMMY FLORES

STACKPOLE
BOOKS

Guilford, Connecticut

Stackpole Books
An imprint of The Rowman & Littlefield Publishing Group, Inc.
Distributed by
NATIONAL BOOK NETWORK
800-462-6420

British Library Cataloguing in Publication Information
Available

Library of Congress Cataloging-in-Publication Data

Names: Flores, Tammy, author.
Title: Crocheted hoods & cowls : 20 enchanting designs for women,
    7 adorable animal hoods for kids / Tammy Flores.
Other titles: Crocheted hoods and cowls
Description: Guilford, Connecticut : Stackpole Books, [2018] |
    Includes index.
Identifiers: LCCN 2018010335 (print) | LCCN 2018016295 (ebook) |
    ISBN 9780811767811 (e-book) | ISBN 9780811717182 (paperback.
    : alk. paper)
Subjects: LCSH: Hoods (Headgear) | Cowls (Neckwear) | Crocheting--
    Patterns.
Classification: LCC TT825 (ebook) | LCC TT825 .F57 2018 (print) | DDC
    746.43/4--dc23
LC record available at https://lccn.loc.gov/2018010335

For my mom—my biggest fan.
Also for my daughters, Lisa and
Olivia, and my husband, Steve.
You guys are my world.

Contents

Adult Hoods, Cowls, and Scarves

Animal Hoods

Adult Hoods, Cowls, and Scarves

Cluster Stitch Hood

Cluster Stitch Hood

*T*he amazing texture of this crochet hood is one of its best features! It's incredibly cozy to wear, but also has a unique and sophisticated style.

FINISHED MEASUREMENTS
Circumference: 30 in./76.2 cm
Height from top of hood to bottom edge of cowl:
    15 in./38.1 cm

YARN
Lion Brand Yarn Lion's Pride Woolspun (80% acrylic/
    20% wool, 127 yd./116.1 m and 3.5 oz./100 g per
    skein), or any #5 bulky weight yarn

    » 3 skeins Charcoal

HOOK AND OTHER SUPPLIES
» Size K-10.5 (6.5 mm) crochet hook
» Yarn needle

GAUGE
Approximately 1½–2 sts in stitch pattern (cluster
    stitch, sc) = 1 in./2.5 cm
Adjust hook size if necessary to obtain gauge.

SPECIAL STITCH
Cluster st: (Yo, insert hook into next st, pull up a loop,
    yo and pull through 2 loops on hook) 2 times, yo
    and pull through remaining loops on hook.

NOTE
» The cowl is worked in the round, but with turning
    after the join so that you work on the front and the
    back. Work around, join your work, and then turn
    to work the next round.

Instructions

COWL SECTION

Ch 54. Being careful not to twist the chain, join into a circle.

Round 1 (RS): Ch 1. Cluster st in first ch, sc in next ch, *cluster st in next ch, sc in next ch; repeat from * around. Join.

Round 2 (WS): Ch 1, turn. Sc in each st around. Join.

Round 3: Ch 1, turn. *Cluster st in next st, sc in next st; repeat from * around. Join.

Rounds 4–9: Rep rounds 2–3.

Fasten off.

HOOD SECTION

You will now begin working in rows, turning the work after each one.

» With WS facing and beginning at the seam where you fastened off, count 24 sts to the right and join yarn.

Row 1 (WS): Ch 1. Sc in same st, *sc in next st; repeat from * across for 48 sts total.

Row 2 (RS): Ch 1, turn. Cluster st in first st, sc in next st, *cluster st in next st, sc in next st; repeat from * across.

Repeat rows 1–2 until hood measures 9½ in./24 cm (desired height).

Fasten off, leaving a long tail to sew hood seam.

Using a yarn needle and the long tail left from fastening off, sew the hood seam using a basic whipstitch or a stitch of your choice.

Slanted Shells Snood

Slanted Shells Snood

This elegant crochet snood has a comfy and casual style. The extra-long cowl can be worn long as a scarf or wrapped twice for a cozy hood and accessory.

FINISHED MEASUREMENTS
9 in./22.9 cm tall x 60 in./152.4 cm long

YARN
Loops & Threads Charisma Tweed (100% acrylic, 93 yd./85 m and 3 oz./85 g per skein), or any #5 bulky weight yarn

» 4 skeins Blue

HOOK AND OTHER SUPPLIES
» Size P/Q (15 mm) crochet hook
» Yarn needle

GAUGE
Approximately 2 sts in hdc = 1 in./2.5 cm
Adjust hook size if necessary to obtain gauge.

Instructions

Ch 120.

Being careful not to twist chain, join into a circle.

Round 1: Ch 1. (Sc, hdc, dc) in same st, sk 2 sts, *(sc, hdc, dc) in next st, sk 2 sts; repeat from * around. Join to first st.

Repeat round 1 until piece measures approximately 9–10 in./22.9–25.4 cm.

Fasten off.

Cozy Cable Hood

Cozy Cable Hood

An elegant, chunky cable details the front of this cozy hooded cowl. Wear the hood up on those truly chilly days, or down as a comfy accessory.

FINISHED MEASUREMENTS
Circumference: 28 in./71.1 cm
Height from top of hood to bottom edge of cowl:
   21 in./53.3 cm

YARN
Loops & Threads Cozy Wool (50% wool/50% acrylic, 90 yd./82.3 m and 4.5 oz./127 g per skein), or any #6 super-bulky weight yarn

» 3 skeins Pewter

HOOK AND OTHER SUPPLIES
» Size N/P-15 (10 mm) crochet hook
» Yarn needle

GAUGE
Approximately 1½ sts in dc = 1 in./2.5 cm
Adjust hook size if necessary to obtain gauge.

SPECIAL STITCHES
Front Post Treble Crochet (fptr): Yo twice, insert hook from front to back to front around post of corresponding stitch below, yo and pull up loop (yo, draw through 2 loops on hook) 3 times.
6cable: Fptr in the 4th, 5th, and 6th st from hook, reach in front of the sts just made, fptr in the 1st, 2nd, and 3rd skipped sts.

Instructions

COWL SECTION

Ch 44. Being careful not to twist the chain, join into a
    circle.
Round 1: Ch 1. Dc in each ch around. Join. (44 sts)
Round 2: Ch 1. Dc in next 19 sts, 6cable, dc in next 19
    sts. Join.
Rounds 3–5: Ch 1. Dc in next 19 sts, fpdc around next
    6 sts, dc in next 19 sts. Join.
Repeat rounds 2–5 two more times, ending with a
    round 5.
Fasten off.

HOOD SECTION

You will now begin working in rows, and turning the
work after each one.

Attach yarn to the stitch directly to the left of the
    cable.
Row 1 (RS): Ch 1. Dc in same st, dc in next 16 sts,
    (dc2tog) twice, dc in next 17 sts. (36 sts)
Row 2 (WS): Ch 1, turn. Dc in same st, dc in next 6 sts,
    dc2tog, dc in next 7 sts, (dc2tog) twice, dc in next
    7 sts, dc2tog, dc in next 7 sts. (32 sts)
Row 3 (RS): Ch 1, turn. Dc in each st across.
Repeat row 3 until the hood measures 10 in./25.4 cm
    (or desired height).
Fasten off, leaving a long tail to sew hood seam.
Using a yarn needle and the long tail left from fas-
    tening off, sew the hood seam using a basic whip-
    stitch or a stitch of your choice.

Knit-Look Snood

Knit-Look Snood

This easy-to-crochet snood features a fun stitch that resembles a knit fabric on one side and a pretty textured stitch on the other. Wear it on either side for style and variety.

Right side

FINISHED MEASUREMENTS
30 in./76.2 cm around x 18 in./45.7 cm tall

YARN
Loops & Threads Cozy Wool (50% wool/50% acrylic, 90 yd./82.3 m and 4.5 oz/127 g per skein), or any #6 super-bulky weight yarn

» 3 skeins Stone

HOOK AND OTHER SUPPLIES
» Size P/Q (15 mm) crochet hook
» Yarn needle

GAUGE
Approximately 1½–2 sts in stitch pattern (single crochet in back loop only) = 1 in./2.5 cm
Adjust hook size if necessary to obtain gauge.

NOTE
» The chain 1 stitches at the beginning of rounds do count as a stitch. When joining at the end of rounds, join to BLO of the beginning chain 1.

Wrong side

Instructions

Ch 50.

Being careful not to twist the chain, join to form a circle.

Round 1: Ch 1, *sc in next ch; repeat from * around. Join to BLO of first st.

Round 2: Ch 1, sc in BLO of each st around. Join to BLO of first st.

Repeat round 2 until snood measures 18 in./45.7 cm (or desired length).

Fasten off.

Linen Stitch Hood

Linen Stitch Hood

This cute hooded cowl makes a perfect fall accessory and is just right for those slightly cooler days or evenings. It features a lovely, subtle linen stitch design that's fun to make and pretty to wear.

FINISHED MEASUREMENTS
Circumference: 30 in./76.2 cm
Height from top of hood to bottom edge of cowl:
21 in./53.3 cm

YARN
Lion Brand Yarn Lion's Pride Woolspun (80% acrylic/20% wool, 127 yd./116.1 m and 3.5 oz./ 100 g per skein), or any #5 bulky weight yarn

» 3 skeins Cranberry

HOOK AND OTHER SUPPLIES
» Size K-10.5 (6.5 mm) crochet hook
» Yarn needle

GAUGE
2½–3 sts in linen stitch = 1 in./2.5 cm
Adjust hook size if necessary to obtain gauge.

Instructions

COWL SECTION

Ch 26.

Row 1: Sc in 2nd ch from hook and in each ch across.

Row 2: Ch 1, turn. Sc in first st, ch 1, sk next st, *sc in next st, ch 1, sk next st; repeat from * across to end, sc in last st.

Row 3: Ch 1, turn. Sc in first ch-1 sp, ch 1, *sc in next ch-1 sp, ch 1; repeat from * across, sc in last st.

Repeat row 3 until piece measures 30 in./76.2 cm, or desired height around of cowl.

Fasten off, leaving a long tail to sew cowl seam.

Bring the two short ends together. Sew them together using the long tail left from fastening off and with a basic whipstitch or stitch of your choice.

Lay the cowl flat with the seam at the back. Using the back seam to find the center of the front, measure 2 in./5.1 cm to the right and mark the stitch. Next, measure 2 in./5.1 cm to the left and join yarn to begin the hood.

HOOD SECTION

Row 1 (RS): Ch 1. Work 49 sc evenly around the edge of the cowl, between where the yarn was joined and the stitch that was marked.

Row 2 (WS): Ch 1, turn. *Sc in next st, ch 1, sk next st; repeat from * across. Sc in last st.

Row 3: Ch 1, turn. *Sc in next ch 1 sp, ch 1; repeat from * across, sc in last st.

Repeat row 3 until the hood measures 10–11 in./25.4–27.9 cm (or desired height).

Fasten off, leaving a long tail to sew hood seam.

Using a yarn needle and the long tail left from fastening off, sew the hood seam using a basic whipstitch, or a stitch of your choice.

Puff Stitch Snood

Puff Stitch Snood

*L*uxurious, *cozy,* and *opulent* are the perfect words to describe this elegant snood! It's made with a super-bulky yarn and a huge crochet hook, so it's an ideal make-it-today-wear-it-to-night kind of project.

FINISHED MEASUREMENTS
18 in./45.7 cm tall x 32 in./81.3 cm long

YARN

Lion Brand Yarn Wool-Ease Thick & Quick (80% acrylic/20% wool; 106 yd./96.9 m and 6 oz./170 g per skein), or any #6 super-bulky weight yarn

» 3 skeins Gemstone Metallic

HOOK AND OTHER SUPPLIES

» Size P/Q (15 mm) crochet hook
» Yarn needle

GAUGE

Approximately ½ st in puff st = 1 in./2.5 cm
Adjust hook size if necessary to obtain gauge.

SPECIAL STITCH

Puff Stitch: (Yo, insert hook into stitch, pull up a loop) 3 times, yo, pull hook through all loops, ch 1 to secure.

Instructions

Ch 34. Without twisting the chain, join into a circle.

Round 1: Ch 1. Puff st in first ch, sk next ch, *puff st in next ch, sk next ch; repeat from * around. Join. (17 puff sts)

Round 2: Sl st into first ch-1 space (this is the chain 1 that was used to secure the puff stitch), ch 1. Puff st in same sp, *puff st in next ch-1 sp; repeat from * around. Join.

Repeat round 2 until cowl measures 18 in./45.7 cm, or until you run out of yarn.

Fasten off.

Herringbone Hooded Scarf

Herringbone Hooded Scarf

The gorgeous textured stitch design of this hooded scarf has an elegant and complex appearance, but it is very easy to crochet. The scarf also includes cozy little pockets to keep your hands warm!

FINISHED MEASUREMENTS
Scarf: 60 in./152.4 cm long x 8 in./20.3 cm wide
Height from top of hood to bottom edge of cowl: 21 in./53.3 cm

YARN
Lion Brand Yarn Lion's Pride Woolspun (80% acrylic/20% wool; 127 yd./116.1 m and 3.5 oz./100 g per skein), or any #5 bulky weight yarn

» 3 skeins Taupe

HOOK AND OTHER SUPPLIES
» Size K-10.5 (6.5 mm) crochet hook
» Yarn needle

GAUGE
Approximately 2½ sts in herringbone dc = 1 in./2.5 cm
Adjust hook size if necessary to obtain gauge.

SPECIAL STITCH
Herringbone Double Crochet (herringbone dc):
Yo and insert hook into next stitch, yo and pull through the stitch and the first loop on hook, yo and pull through one loop on hook, yo and pull through remaining loops on hook.

Instructions

SCARF SECTION
Ch 20.
Row 1: Herringbone dc in 4th ch from hook, *herringbone dc in next ch; repeat from * across.
Row 2: Ch 1, turn. Herringbone dc in each st across.
Repeat row 2 until scarf measures approximately 76 in./193 cm long.
Fasten off.

POCKETS
Fold one end of the scarf up to make a pocket that measures approximately 8 in./20.3 cm deep. Using matching yarn, sew the two side seams for the pocket.
Repeat on the other end of the scarf.

HOOD SECTION
Measure approximately 19 in./48.3 cm, along the long edge of the scarf, from the bottom edge of a pocket.
Attach yarn with a slip stitch.
Row 1 (RS): Work 44 herringbone dc evenly over the next 22 in./55.9 cm. (44 sts)
(You should have approximately 19 in./48.3 cm of the scarf edge left, after these stitches are worked.)
Row 2 (WS): Ch 1, turn. Herringbone dc in each st across. (44 sts)
Repeat row 2 until hood measures 12 in./30.5 cm (or desired height).
Fasten off, leaving a long tail to sew hood seam.
Using a yarn needle and the long tail left from fastening off, sew the hood seam using a basic whipstitch, or a stitch of your choice.

Chunky Ribbed Hood

Chunky Ribbed Hood

This darling hooded cowl has a definite pixie feel! It features a cozy yarn, a unique stitch design, and a cute, pointy hood.

FINISHED MEASUREMENTS
Circumference: 26 in./66 cm
Height from top of head to bottom edge of cowl: 18 in./45.7 cm

YARN
Lion Brand Yarn Wool-Ease Tonal (80% acrylic/20% wool, 124 yd./116.7 m and 4 oz./113 g per skein), or any #5 bulky weight yarn

» 3 skeins Charcoal

HOOK AND OTHER SUPPLIES
» Size K-10.5 (6.5 mm) crochet hook
» Yarn needle
» 5 1½-in./3.8-cm buttons

GAUGE
Approximately 2 sts in hdc rib = 1 in./2.5 cm
Adjust hook size if necessary to obtain gauge.

SPECIAL STITCH
Half double crochet ribbed stitch: Work a hdc into the "third" loop of the hdc below. This "third" loop sits at the front of the stitch, below the two regular loops at the top of the stitch.

NOTE

» Each row, beginning with row 2, will be worked as half double crochet ribbed stitch. The only stitches that will not be worked in this special stitch will be some of the edge stitches (which will be indicated in the directions). For those stitches, work into the top two loops of the stitch, as you would for a normal hdc stitch.

Instructions

COWL SECTION

Ch 61.

Row 1: Hdc in 2nd chain from hook, *hdc in next ch; repeat from * across. (60 sts)

Row 2: Ch 1, turn. Work hdc rib across until the last st. Work the last hdc into the two top loops of the edge stitch. (60 sts)

Rows 2–17: Repeat row 2.

Fasten off.

Attach 5 buttons along one short end of the cowl. The space in between the stitches on the other short side of the cowl will act as the buttonholes. Make sure to use buttons that are large enough so that they will not slip out when being worn.

Button the cowl shut to find hood placement.

Be sure to continue to work in the stitch pattern by making your hdc stitches into the "third loop," so whichever side your "third loop" is on (RS or WS), continue on that side.

HOOD SECTION

Find the back center stitch of the cowl and count 25 stitches toward the right, front side of the cowl.

Attach the yarn with a slip stitch.

Row 1: Ch 1. Working in hdc rib, work a hdc in the same st that you joined to, and in the next 48 sts. Work a hdc into the two top loops of the next st. (50 sts)

Row 2: Ch 1, turn. Working in hdc rib, work a hdc in the same st that you joined to, and in the next 48 sts. Work a hdc into the two top loops of the next st. (50 sts)

Repeat row 2 until hood measures 9–10 in./22.9–25.4 cm (or desired height).

Fasten off, leaving a long tail to sew hood seam.

Using a yarn needle and the long tail left from fastening off, sew the hood seam using a basic whip-stitch, or a stitch of your choice.

Faux Cable Snood

Faux Cable Snood

Incredibly warm and cozy perfectly describes this crochet snood! It features a gorgeous, textured stitch that's also easy to work. If you enjoy a project that appears to be more difficult than it really is, then this one is for you!

FINISHED MEASUREMENTS
Circumference: 28 in./71.1 cm
Height: 18 in./45.7 cm

YARN
Lion Brand Yarn Lion's Pride Woolspun (80% acrylic/20% wool, 127 yd./116.1 m and 3.5 oz./ 100 g per skein), or any #5 bulky weight yarn

» 3 skeins Orchid

HOOK AND OTHER SUPPLIES
» Size K-10.5 (6.5 mm) crochet hook
» Yarn needle

GAUGE
Approximately 2 sts in stitch pattern = 1 in./2.5 cm
Adjust hook size if necessary to obtain gauge.

NOTE

» Beginning with round 3, you will always be working the double crochet stitches into the top of the front post double crochet stitches from the previous round, and you will work the front post double crochet stitches around the double crochet stitches from the previous round.

Instructions

Ch 58.

Row 1: Dc in 3rd ch from hook, *dc in next ch; repeat from * across. (56 sts)

Being careful not to twist the length of stitches, join to the first stitch with a slip stitch. You will now be working in rounds.

Round 2: Ch 1. Dc in same st, fpdc around next st, *dc in next st, fpdc around next st; repeat from * around. Join.

Round 3: Ch 1. Fpdc around same st, dc in next st, *fpdc around next st, dc in next st; repeat from * around. Join.

Repeat rounds 2 and 3 until snood measures 18 in./ 45.7 cm, or until you run out of yarn.

Fasten off.

Pretty Hooded Scarf

Pretty Hooded Scarf

This simple and pretty design is incredibly easy to crochet and a joy to wear! The textured stitch gives it tons of dimension, and the style is suitable for either casual or dressy wear.

FINISHED MEASUREMENTS
18 in./45.7 cm tall x 28 in./71.1 cm long

YARN
Lion Brand Yarn Wool-Ease Chunky (80% acrylic/20% wool; 153 yd./140 m and 5 oz./140 g per skein), or any #5 bulky weight yarn

» 3 skeins Eggplant

HOOK AND OTHER SUPPLIES
» Size L-11 (8 mm) crochet hook
» Yarn needle

GAUGE
Approximately 2 sts in sc in BLO = 1 in./2.5 cm
Adjust hook size if necessary to obtain gauge.

Instructions

SCARF SECTION

Ch 123.

Row 1 (RS): Sc in 2nd ch from hook, *sc in next ch; repeat from * across. (122 sts)

Row 2 (WS): Ch 1, turn. Sc in BLO of same st, *sc in BLO of next st; repeat from * across to last st, sc in both loops of last st.

Repeat row 2 until scarf measures 8–10 in./20.3–25.4 cm wide.

Fasten off.

HOOD SECTION

Position the scarf so that it is lying lengthwise with the last row worked at the top.

Count 40 stitches in from the right end of the scarf and join the yarn with a slip stitch.

Row 1 (RS): Ch 1. Sc in BLO of same st, sc in BLO of next 40 sts, sc in both loops of next st. (42 sts)

Row 2 (WS): Ch 1, turn. Sc in BLO of same st, *sc in BLO of next st; repeat from * across to last st, sc in both loops of last st.

Repeat row 2 until hood measures 14 in./35.6 cm (or desired height).

Fasten off, leaving a long tail to sew hood seam.

HOOD SEAM

Using a yarn needle and the long tail left from fastening off, sew the hood seam using a basic whipstitch, or a stitch of your choice.

Easy & Elegant Snood

Easy & Elegant Snood

If you're looking for a classic and elegant accessory that's easy to make, then this is it! This cozy snood is made entirely with one stitch and is a perfect beginner's project. It's great for wearing with jeans and a T-shirt, or for dressing up an outfit for the office.

FINISHED MEASUREMENTS
Circumference: 39 in./99.1 cm
Height from top to bottom: 20 in./50.8 cm

YARN
I Love This Chunky! Yarn (100% acrylic, 109 yd./102.6 m and 3.5 oz./100 g per skein), or any #5 bulky weight yarn

» 3 skeins French Lilac

HOOK AND OTHER SUPPLIES
» Size L-11 (8 mm) crochet hook
» Yarn needle

GAUGE
Approximately 1½–2 sts in stitch pattern (half double crochet) = 1 in./2.5 cm
Adjust hook size if necessary to obtain gauge.

NOTE

» This snood is worked in continuous rounds, without joining. At the beginning of round 2, place a marker to mark the first stitch. When you reach the end of each round, move the marker up to mark the beginning of the next round.

Instructions

Ch 70. Being careful not to twist the chain, join into a circle.

Round 1: Ch 1. Hdc in each ch around. Place marker to mark beginning of next round and move it up as you finish each round. *Do not join.*

Round 2: Hdc in each st around.

Repeat round 2 until you have approximately 12 in./ 30.5 cm of yarn left.

Join the last stitch that you work to the next one with a slip st and fasten off.

Scalloped Shells Snood

Scalloped Shells Snood

The casual yet elegant style of this snood makes it a fabulous accessory for everyday wear. It pairs well with blue jeans and a sweater and with dressier outfits, too.

FINISHED MEASUREMENTS
Circumference: 32 in./81.3 cm
Height from top to bottom: 18 in./45.7 cm

YARN
Lion Brand Yarn Lion's Pride Woolspun (80% acrylic/ 20% wool, 127 yd./116.1 m and 3.5 oz./100 g per skein), or any #5 bulky weight yarn

» 3 skeins Evergreen

HOOK AND OTHER SUPPLIES
» Size K-10.5 (6.5 mm) crochet hook
» Yarn needle

GAUGE
Approximately 2–2½ sts in stitch pattern = 1 in./ 2.5 cm
Adjust hook size if necessary to obtain gauge.

Instructions

Ch 72. Being careful not to twist the chain, join into a circle.

Round 1: Ch 1. Dc in same ch, *dc in next ch; repeat from * around. Join. (72 sts)

Round 2: Ch 3 (counts as a dc). Dc in same sp, ch 1, 2dc in same sp, sk 2 sts, dc in next st, sk 2 sts, *(2dc, ch 1, 2dc) in next st, sk 2 sts, dc in next st, sk 2 sts; repeat from * around. Join to top of chain 3. Slip st in next st, slip st in next ch 1 sp.

Repeat round 2 until cowl/hood measures 18 in./45.7 cm or desired length.

Fasten off.

Double Wrap
Hooded Cowl

Double Wrap Hooded Cowl

*T*he simplicity of this hooded cowl makes it incredibly easy to wear and perfect for just about any type of outfit! Wear the cowl wrapped twice for added warmth or wear it long for a more casual look.

FINISHED MEASUREMENTS
Circumference: 56 in./142.2 cm
Height from top of hood to bottom edge of cowl:
    16 in./40.6 cm

YARN
Loops & Threads Cozy Wool (50% wool/50% acrylic, 90 yd./82.3 m and 4.5 oz./127 g per skein), or any #6 super-bulky weight yarn

   » 3 skeins Mushroom

HOOK AND OTHER SUPPLIES
   » Size P/Q (15 mm) crochet hook
   » Yarn needle

GAUGE
Approximately 1½ sts in hdc = 1 in./2.5 cm
Adjust hook size if necessary to obtain gauge.

Instructions

COWL SECTION

Ch 80. Being careful not to twist the chain, join into a circle.

Round 1: Ch 1. Hdc in same ch, *hdc in next ch; repeat from * around. Join. (80 sts)

» Each Row 2 will be made by working into the extra loop that sits at the front of the stitch and the front loop at the top of the stitch. This leaves the back loop at the top of the stitch unworked.

Round 2: Ch 1. Hdc in same st, *half double crochet in next st; repeat from * around. Join. (80 sts)

Rounds 3–7: Repeat round 2.
 Fasten off.

HOOD SECTION

You will now begin working in rows, turning the work after each one.

Place the "joining seam" at the back.

Count 14 stitches to the left of center seam, and attach yarn. You will begin working the hood on the right side (outside).

Row 1 (RS): Ch 1. Hdc in 2 top loops of same st, and in next 27 sts. (28 sts)

Row 2 (WS): Row 2 will be made by working into the extra loop that sits at the front of the stitch and the back loop at the top of the stitch. This leave the front loop at the top of the stitch unworked.) Ch 1, turn. Hdc in same st, hdc in next 27 sts. (28 sts)

Row 3: Ch 1, turn. Hdc in 2 top loops of same st, and in next 27 sts.

Repeat rows 2 and 3 until hood measures 10–11 in./ 25.4–27.9 cm tall (or desired height).

Fasten off, leaving a long tail to sew the hood seam.

Using a yarn needle and the long tail left from fastening off, sew the hood seam using a basic whipstitch, or a stitch of your choice.

Hooded Triangle Cowl

Hooded Triangle Cowl

*a*dd a little extra warmth to your fall and winter outfits with this pretty hooded cowl. The fringe trim gives it a little extra detail and whimsy!

FINISHED MEASUREMENTS
Circumference: 30 in./76.2 cm
Height from top of hood to bottom of triangle front: 30 in./76.2 cm

YARN
Loops & Threads Charisma Heather (100% acrylic, 93 yd./85 m and 3.5 oz./100 g per skein), or any #5 bulky weight yarn

» 3 skeins Denim

HOOK AND OTHER SUPPLIES
» Size M/N-13 (9 mm) crochet hook
» Yarn needle

GAUGE
Approximately 1½–2 sts in dc = 1 in./2.5 cm
Adjust hook size if necessary to obtain gauge.

NOTE
» To be sure that you have enough yarn left over to add fringe to the cowl, cut the fringe pieces first, before crocheting the hooded cowl. The cowl shown has approximately 30 fringes around the triangle. Each cut piece was 12 in./30.5 cm, resulting in a 6-in./15.2-cm fringe.

Instructions

COWL SECTION

You will be working in rounds for this part of the cowl.

Ch 50. Being careful not to twist the chain, join into a circle.

Round 1: Ch 1. Dc in same ch, *dc in next ch; repeat from * around. Join. (50 sts)

Rounds 2–7: Ch 2. Dc in each st around. Join. (50 sts)

» You will now begin working in rows, rather than rounds.

Row 1: Ch 1. Dc in next 25 sts, leaving the remaining 25 sts unworked. (25 sts)

Row 2: Ch 1, turn. Dc in first st, dc2tog, dc in each st until 3 sts remain, dc2tog, dc in last st. Turn. (23 sts)

Repeat row 2 until 5 sts remain.

Next row: Ch 1. Dc in first st, dc3tog, dc in last st. (3 sts)

Fasten off.

HOOD SECTION

You will continue to work in rows, turning the work after each one.

Position the cowl so that the front "triangle" is facing you. Find the approximate front center stitch in the top round of the cowl section.

Count 3 stitches over to the left and attach the yarn with a slip stitch.

Row 1: Ch 1. Dc in same st, dc in next 43 sts. (44 sts)

Row 2: Ch 1, turn. Dc in each st across. (44 sts)

Repeat row 2 until hood section measures approximately 14 in./35.6 cm (or desired height).

Fasten off, leaving a long tail to sew hood seam.

Using a yarn needle and the long tail left from fastening off, sew the hood seam using a basic whipstitch or a stitch of your choice.

FRINGE

Fold a piece of fringe in half and, using a crochet hook, pull the loop end through an edge stitch of the cowl. Now pull the two loose ends of the fringe through the loop and pull to tighten.

Repeat around for all fringe pieces.

Star Stitch Hooded Scarflette

Star Stitch Hooded Scarflette

The little scarflette is super cute and a great option for those who don't like an oversized scarf. It also features the elegant star stitch throughout the entire project, making it a joy to crochet and to wear!

FINISHED MEASUREMENTS
18 in./45.7 cm tall x 40 in./101.6 cm long

YARN
I Love This Yarn! (100% acrylic, 355 yd./324.6 m and 7 oz./199 g per skein), or any other #4 worsted weight yarn

» 2 skeins #130 Dark Olive

HOOK AND OTHER SUPPLIES
» Size I-9 (5.5 mm) crochet hook
» Yarn needle

GAUGE
1½ sts in stitch pattern (star stitch) = 1 in./2.5 cm
Adjust hook size if necessary to obtain gauge.

Instructions

SCARF SECTION

Ch 119.

Row 1: Insert hook into 2nd chain from hook and pull up a loop, insert hook into 3rd chain from hook and pull up a loop, insert hook into 4th chain from hook and pull up a loop, insert hook into 5th chain from hook and pull up a loop, insert hook into 6th chain from hook and pull up a loop, yo and pull through all 6 loops on hook, ch 1, *insert hook into "eye" of previous star st and pull up a loop, insert hook into "side" st of previous start st and pull up a loop, insert hook into "base" st of previous star st and pull up a loop, (insert hook into next st and pull up a loop) 2 times, yo and pull yarn through all 6 loops on hook, ch 1; repeat from * across. Work a hdc in the last chain (included with the last star stitch).

Row 2: Ch 2, turn (counts as first st), *2hdc in "eye" of next star st; repeat from * across to last st, hdc in last st.

Row 3: Ch 3, turn. Insert hook into 2nd chain from hook and pull up a loop, insert hook into 3rd chain from hook and pull up a loop, insert hook into the first st and pull up a loop, (insert hook into next st and pull up a loop) 2 times, yo and pull yarn through all 6 loops on hook, ch 1, *insert hook into "eye" of previous star st and pull up a loop, insert hook into "side" st of previous star st and pull up a loop, insert hook into "base" st of previous star st and pull up a loop, (insert hook into next st and pull up a loop) 2 times, yo and pull yarn through all 6 loops on hook, ch 1; repeat from * across, hdc in edge st (the turning chain 2 from the previous row).

Repeat rows 2 and 3 until pieces measures 6 in./ 15.2 cm.

Fasten off.

HOOD SECTION

Ch 71.

Row 1: Insert hook into 2nd chain from hook and pull up a loop, insert hook into 3rd chain from hook and pull up a loop, insert hook into 4th chain from hook and pull up a loop, insert hook into 5th chain from hook and pull up a loop, insert hook into 6th chain from hook and pull up a loop, yo and pull through all 6 loops on hook, ch 1, *insert hook into "eye" of previous star st and pull up a loop, insert hook into "side" st of previous star st and pull up a loop, insert hook into "base" st of previous star st and pull up a loop, (insert hook into next st and pull up a loop) 2 times, yo and pull yarn through all 6 loops on hook, ch 1; repeat from * across to last chain, hdc in last chain (included with the last star stitch).

Row 2: Ch 2, turn (counts as first st), *2hdc in "eye" of next star st; repeat from * across to last st, hdc in last st.

Row 3: Ch 3, turn. Insert hook into 2nd chain from hook and pull up a loop, insert hook into 3rd chain from hook and pull up a loop, insert hook into the first st and pull up a loop, (insert hook into next st and pull up a loop) 2 times, yo and pull yarn through all 6 loops on hook, ch 1, *insert hook into "eye" of previous star st and pull up a loop, insert hook into "side" st of previous star st and pull up a loop, insert hook into "base" st of previous star st and pull up a loop, (insert hook into next st and pull up a loop) 2 times, yo and pull yarn through all 6 loops on hook, ch 1; repeat from * across, hdc in edge st (the turning ch 2 from the previous row).

Repeat rows 2 and 3 until hood measures 13–14 in./ 33–35.6 cm.

Fasten off, leaving a long tail to sew hood seam.

Using a yarn needle and the long tail left from fastening off, sew the hood seam using a basic whipstitch, or a stitch of your choice.

ATTACH HOOD TO SCARFLETTE

Once hood seam is sewn, line up the center back of the hood to the center of one long edge of the scarf.

Using matching yarn and a yarn needle, sew the hood to the scarf using a basic whipstitch, or a stitch of your choice. You can also use a single crochet stitch, or a slip stitch, to sew the hood to the scarf.

Enchanting Pixie Hood

Enchanting Pixie Hood

This enchanting pixie hood features a unique textured stitch and is easy to wear with the button-on band. Such a fun fall accessory!

FINISHED MEASUREMENTS
Circumference: 20 in./50.8 cm
Height from top of hood to bottom: 14 in./35.6 cm

YARN
Lion Brand Yarn Vanna's Choice (100% acrylic, 145 yd./132.6 m and 3 oz./85 g per skein), or any #4 worsted weight yarn

» 2 skeins Silver Heather

HOOK AND OTHER SUPPLIES
» Size H (5 mm) crochet hook
» Yarn needle
» 1 button (1½ in./3.8 cm)

GAUGE
3 sts in dc = 1 in./2.5 cm
Adjust hook size if necessary to obtain gauge.

Instructions

HOOD

Ch 32.

Row 1 (RS): Sc in 2nd ch from hook, sc in each ch across. (31 sts)

Row 2: Ch 2, turn. Dc in first st, *bpdc in next st, dc in next st; repeat from * across. (31 sts)

Row 3: Ch 2, turn. Dc in first st, *fpdc in next st, dc in next st; repeat from * across. (31 sts)

Repeat rows 2 and 3 until piece measures approximately 25 in./63.5 cm long.

Last row: (Make a chain 1, instead of a chain 2, at the end of the row before this.) Sc in each st across.

Fasten off, leaving a long tail to sew hood seam.

Fold the piece in half and, beginning at the fold, sew *one* open edge together with the long yarn tail and a yarn needle.

The seam that you just sewed is the back of the hood. The "longer/taller" opening is the front of the hood. The remaining edge is the neck edge.

NECK BAND

» The back seam will be in the center of this edge. When working the stitches around, use the "seam" stitch as a regular stitch. Including that, there will be 50 sts.

Attach the yarn to the front, left bottom edge.

Row 1 (RS): Ch 1. *Sc in next 4 sts, sc2tog; repeat from * across. Ch 1, turn. (50 sts)

Rows 2–5: Sc in each st across. (50 sts)

Do not fasten off.

BUTTON BAND

Turn the work so that you will be working along the short end of the band that was just made.

For this button band, the chain 1 stitches will be used as a stitch.

Row 1 (RS): Ch 1. Sc 5 sts evenly across the edge of the neck band. Ch 1, turn.

Rows 2–9: Skip the first st, *Sc in next st; repeat from * across, sc in turning chain from previous row. Ch 1, turn. (5 sts)

Row 10: (Buttonhole row) Skip the first st, sc in next st, ch 2, skip 2 sts, sc in next st, sc in turning chain from previous row. Ch 1, turn. (5 sts).

Row 11: Skip the first st, sc in next st, sc in each of 2 chains, sc in next st, sc in turning chain from previous row. Ch 1, turn. (5 sts)

Row 12: Skip the first st, *sc in next st; repeat from * across, sc in turning chain from previous row. Ch 1, turn. (5 sts)

Row 13: Skip the first st, *sc in next st; repeat from * across, sc in turning chain from previous row.

Fasten off.

Weave in ends.

Attach a button to the bottom corner of the hood, and slip through the buttonhole.

Easy Hooded Cowl

Easy Hooded Cowl

The cozy, oversize style of this hooded cowl makes it a joy to wear. It can be perfectly paired with your favorite sweater and blue jeans or added to your outdoor attire on those truly chilly days.

FINISHED MEASUREMENTS
Circumference: 30 in./76.2 cm
Height from top of hood to bottom edge of cowl: 22 in./55.9 cm

YARN
Lion Brand Yarn Wool-Ease Thick & Quick (80% acrylic/20% wool, 106 yd./96.9 m and 6 oz./170 g per skein), or any #6 super-bulky weight yarn

» 3 skeins Fisherman

HOOK AND OTHER SUPPLIES
» Size N/P-15 (10 mm) crochet hook
» Yarn needle

GAUGE
Approximately 1½ sts in dc = 1 in./2.5 cm
Adjust hook size if necessary to obtain gauge.

Instructions

COWL SECTION

Ch 44. Being careful not to twist the chain, join into a
    circle.
Round 1: Ch 1. Dc in same ch, *dc in next ch; repeat
    from * around. Join. (44 sts)
Rounds 2–10: Ch 1. Dc in same st, *dc in next st;
    repeat from * around. Join.
Fasten off.

HOOD SECTION

» Placing the "joining seam" at the back, you will
    now begin working in rows, turning the work after
    each one.

Beginning at the stitch that you fastened off with,
    count 20 stitches to the right. Attach yarn with a
    slip stitch.
Row 1: Ch 1. Dc in same st, dc in next 39 sts. (40 sts)
Row 2: Ch 1, turn. Dc in each st across. (40 sts)
Repeat row 2 until hood measures 12 in./ 30.5 cm (or
    desired height).
Fasten off, leaving a long tail to sew hood seam.
Using a yarn needle and the long tail left from fas-
    tening off, sew the hood seam using a basic whip-
    stitch or a stitch of your choice.

Cross-Stitch
Hooded Scarf

Cross-Stitch Hooded Scarf

*T*his pretty hooded scarf features a cross-over stitch design and an easy-to-wear style. Add the optional pom-pom for a little extra embellishment!

FINISHED MEASUREMENTS

9 in./22.9 cm wide x 60 in./132.1 cm long

YARN

I Love This Chunky! Yarn (100% acrylic, 109 yd./99.7 m and 3.5 oz./100 g per skein), or any other #5 bulky weight yarn

» 4 skeins Pearl Gray

Optional: Worsted weight yarn for pom-pom.

HOOK AND OTHER SUPPLIES

» Size K-10.5 (6.5 mm) crochet hook
» Yarn needle
» Optional: Pom-pom maker

GAUGE

2½ sts in cross-stitch pattern = 1 in./2.5 cm
Adjust hook size if necessary to obtain gauge.

SPECIAL STITCH

Dc in skipped stitch: Working over the stitch that you just made, insert your hook into the skipped stitch (just to the right) and work a dc as normal.

Instructions

SCARF SECTION

Ch 24.

Row 1: Dc in 3rd ch from hook, *sk next ch, dc in next ch, dc in skipped ch; repeat from * across, dc in last ch.

Row 2: Ch 1, turn. Skip first st, dc in next st, dc in skipped st, *sk next st, dc in next st, dc in skipped st; repeat from * across.

Row 3: Ch 1, turn. Dc in first st, *sk next st, dc in next st, dc in skipped st; repeat from * across, dc in last st.

Repeat rows 2 and 3 until scarf measures 60 in./152.4 cm (or desired length).

Fasten off.

HOOD SECTION

Fold the scarf in half. Find the center of the scarf, at the fold, and measure 10 in./25.4 cm to the right. Attach the yarn with a slip stitch.

Row 1: Ch 1. Work 42 dc evenly along the edge of the scarf.

» When you are finished, you should have about 20 in./50.8 cm of scarf on each side of the first row of the hood.

Row 2: Ch 1, turn. Dc in first st, *sk next st, dc in next st, dc in skipped st; repeat from * across, dc in last st.

Row 3: Ch 1, turn. Skip first st, dc in next st, dc in skipped st, *sk next st, dc in next st, dc in skipped st; repeat from * across.

Repeat rows 2 and 3 until hood measures 12–13 in./30.5–33 cm (or desired height).

Fasten off, leaving a long tail to sew hood seam.

Using a yarn needle and the long tail left from fastening off, sew the hood seam using a basic whipstitch or a stitch of your choice.

OPTIONAL POM-POM

Using a pom-pom maker (or a method of your choice), make a pom-pom and attach it to the tip of the hood.

Hooded Button Scarf

Hooded Button Scarf

This cute crochet hood features a short wraparound scarf with a button closure. It's made entirely with the well-loved half double crochet stitch, so it's be fun and easy to crochet!

FINISHED MEASUREMENT
20 in./50.8 cm tall x 35 in./88.9 cm long

YARN
Lion Brand Yarn Lion's Pride Woolspun (80% acrylic/20% wool, 127 yd./116.1 m and 3.5 oz./100 g per skein), or any #5 bulky weight yarn

» 3 skeins Oxford Gray

HOOK AND OTHER SUPPLIES
» Size M/N-13 (9 mm) crochet hook
» Yarn needle
» 3 Buttons (1–1½ in./2.5–3.8 cm)

GAUGE
Approximately 2 sts in hdc = 1 in./2.5 cm
Adjust hook size if necessary to obtain gauge.

Instructions

SCARF SECTION

Ch 18.

Row 1: Hdc in 2nd ch from hook, hdc in each ch across. (17 sts)

Row 2: Ch 1, turn. Hdc in each st across. (17 sts)

Repeat row 2 until scarf measures 35 in./81.3 cm. Fasten off.

HOOD SECTION

Lay the scarf lengthwise. Measure 6 in./15.2 cm in from the right short edge and attach yarn.

Row 1: Work hdc stitches evenly across the edge of the scarf until you reach 6 in./15.24 cm before the other end of the scarf. You should have approximately 38–40 stitches. The exact number of stitches is not incredibly important.

Row 2: Ch 1, turn. Hdc in each st across.

Repeat row 2 until hood measures 12–13 in./30.5–33 cm tall.

Fasten off, leaving a long tail to sew hood seam.

Using a yarn needle and the long tail left from fastening off, sew the hood seam using a basic whipstitch, or a stitch of your choice.

BUTTONS

Attach 3 buttons along the long edge, near one end of the scarf. Use the stitches on the other short end of the scarf as the buttonholes to secure closed.

Big Bow Hood

Big Bow Hood

This sweet hooded cowl features a pretty crochet bow at the front and a slightly oversize hood. Cozy and cute!

FINISHED MEASUREMENTS
Circumference: 30 in./76.2 cm
Height from top of hood to bottom edge of cowl: 22 in./55.9 cm

YARN
Lion Brand Yarn Wool-Ease Thick & Quick (80% acrylic/20% wool, 106 yd./ 96.9 m and 6 oz./170 g per skein), or any #6 super-bulky weight yarn

» 3 skeins Oatmeal

A small amount of worsted weight yarn for the bow

WHOOK AND OTHER SUPPLIES
» Size N/P-15 (10 mm) crochet hook
» Size H (5 mm) crochet hook
» Yarn needle

GAUGE
Approximately 1½ sts in stitch pattern = 1 in./2.5 cm
Adjust hook size if necessary to obtain gauge.

NOTE
» The cowl section of this hood may have a slightly visible "seam" where the joining is done at the end of rounds. When the hood is added, this "seam" is positioned toward the back.

Instructions

COWL SECTION

» For every other round, you will be working into the 2 "back-most" loops of the stitch. This means that you will insert the hook into the back loop of the two loops on the top of the stitch and into the "extra third loop" that sits behind the stitch. This will leave the front-most loop of the stitch unworked, giving the cowl its subtle ribbed texture.

With Oatmeal yarn and N/P-15 crochet hook, ch 47.

Row 1: Hdc in 2nd ch from hook, hdc in each ch across. Join to first st to form a circle. (46 sts)

Round 2: Ch 1. * Hdc in the 2 "back-most" loops of same st, hdc in the 2 "back-most" loops of next st; repeat from * around.

Round 3: Ch 1. Hdc in same st, *hdc in next st; repeat from * around until last 2 sts, hdc2tog in last 2 sts. (45 sts)

Repeat rounds 2 and 3 until you have 40 sts.

Fasten off.

HOOD SECTION

Position the cowl so that the slight "seam" is at the back.

Beginning at the fastened-off stitch, count 16 sts to the right toward the front center of the cowl.

Attach yarn with a slip stitch.

Row 1: Ch 1. Hdc in the 2 "back-most" loops of same st, hdc in the 2 "back-most" loops of next 31 sts. (32 sts)

Row 2: Ch 1, turn. Hdc in same st, *hdc in next st; repeat from * around.

Repeat row 2 until hood measures approximately 12 in./30.5 cm.

Fasten off, leaving a long tail to sew hood seam.

Using a yarn needle and the long tail left from fastening off, sew the hood seam using a basic whip-stitch, or a stitch of your choice.

BOW

With worsted weight yarn and size H crochet hook, ch 40. Being careful not to twist the chains, join into a circle.

Round 1: Ch 1. Hdc in same ch, *hdc in next ch; repeat from * around. Join. (40 sts)

» For the remainder of the bow, you will be working in the 2 "back-most" loops of each stitch. Do not work into the extra "third" loop at the front of the stitches.

Rounds 2–12: Ch 1. Hdc in same st, *hdc in next st; repeat from * around. Join.

Fasten off.

TIE

With worsted weight yarn and size H crochet hook, make a chain that is 12–16 in./30.5–40.6 cm long.

Row 1: Sc in 2nd ch from hook, *sc in next ch; repeat from * across.

Fasten off.

Wrap tie around the center of the bow and secure with a basic knot.

Using matching yarn and a yarn needle, sew the bow to the front of the cowl.

Animal Hoods

Kitty Cat

This sweet kitty-cat hood makes a fun and fanciful accessory for the cooler seasons. Purrrfect for any lucky little one!

FINISHED MEASUREMENTS
Circumference: 28 in./71.1 cm
Height from top of hood to bottom edge of cowl:
    20 in./50.8 cm

YARN
Loops & Threads Cozy Wool (50% wool/50% acrylic,
    90 yd./82.3 m and 4.5 oz./127 g per skein), or any
    #6 super-bulky weight yarn

    » 2 skeins Barley
    » 1 skein Mushroom

HOOK AND OTHER SUPPLIES
    » Size M/N-13 (9 mm) crochet hook (for cowl/hood)
    » Size L (8 mm) crochet hook (for ears)
    » Yarn needle

GAUGE
Approximately 1½ sts in hdc = 1 in./2.5 cm using size
    M/N-13 crochet hook
Adjust hook size if necessary to obtain gauge.

Instructions

COWL SECTION

With size M/N-13 crochet hook and Barley, ch 44. Being careful not to twist the chain, join into a circle.

Round 1: Ch 1. Hdc in same ch, *hdc in next ch; repeat from * around. Join. (44 sts)

Rounds 2–9: Ch 1, turn. *Hdc in next st; repeat from * around. Join. (44 sts)

After round 9, piece should measure approximately 7 in./ 17.8 cm.

Round 10: Ch 1. Hdc2tog, *hdc in next 4 sts, hdc2tog; repeat from * around. Join. (36 sts)

Fasten off.

HOOD SECTION

Continue with Barley for the entire hood. You will now begin working in rows, without joining. Place the "joining seam" at the back and attach the yarn to a center stitch at the front of the cowl.

Row 1: Ch 1. Hdc in same st, *hdc in next st; repeat from * across. (36 sts)

Row 2: Ch 1, turn. Hdc in each st across. (36 sts)

Repeat row 2 until hood measures 10–11 in./ 25.4–27.9 cm (or desired height).

Fasten off, leaving a long tail to sew hood seam.

Using a yarn needle and the long tail left from fastening off, sew the hood seam using a basic whipstitch or a stitch of your choice.

Attach Mushroom yarn to any stitch around the edge of the hood opening.

Work 1 round of sc evenly around the hood opening. Fasten off.

EARS (MAKE 2)

With Mushroom and size L crochet hook, ch 2.

Round 1: 3sc in 2nd ch from hook. Join. (3 sts)

Round 2: Ch 1. 2sc in same st,*2sc in next st; repeat from * around. Join. (6 sts)

Round 3: Ch 1. Sc in same st, sc in next st, 2sc in next st, *sc in next 2 sts, 2sc in next st; repeat from * around. Join. (8 sts)

Round 4: Ch 1. Sc in same st, sc in next 2 sts, 2 sc in next st, sc in next 3 sts, 2 sc in next st. Join. (10 sts)

Round 5: Ch 1. Sc in same st, sc in next 3 sts, 2 sc in next st, sc in next 4 sts, 2 sc in next st. Join. (12 sts)

Round 6: Ch 1. Sc in each st around. Join. (12 sts)

Fasten off, leaving a long tail to sew ears to hood. Sew ears to hood.

Dinosaur

*W*hat little boy or girl wouldn't love to wear this fantastic dinosaur hood? Complete with little spikes and a tail, it features a big, cozy yarn for extra warmth. A perfect fall and winter accessory.

FINISHED MEASUREMENTS
Circumference: 28 in./71.1 cm
Height from top of hood spikes to bottom edge of cowl: 21 in./53.3 cm

YARN
Lion Brand Yarn Wool-Ease Thick & Quick for hood (80% acrylic/20% wool, 106 yd./96.9 m and 6 oz./170 g per skein), or any #6 super-bulky weight yarn

» 3 skeins Grass

Loops & Threads Charisma for spikes and tail (100% acrylic, 109 yd./99.7 m and 3.5 oz./100 g per skein), or any #5 bulky weight yarn

» 1 skein Off White

HOOK AND OTHER SUPPLIES

» Size M/N-13 (9 mm) crochet hook (for cowl/hood)
» Size K-10.5 (6.5 mm) crochet hook (for spikes and tail)
» Yarn needle

NOTE

» The chain 1 stitches used in the stitch pattern *do* count as a stitch.

GAUGE

Approximately 1½–2 sts in sc = 1 in./2.5 cm using size M/N-13 crochet hook

Adjust hook size if necessary to obtain gauge.

Instructions

COWL SECTION

Using Wool-Ease Thick & Quick and size M/N-13 crochet hook, ch 50. Being careful not to twist the chain, join into a circle.

Round 1: Ch 1. Sc in same ch, ch 1, skip next ch, *sc in next ch, ch 1, skip next ch; repeat from * around. Join. (50 sts)

Round 2: Ch 1, turn. *Sc in next ch 1 sp, ch 1; repeat from * around. Join. (50 sts)

Rounds 3–12: Repeat round 2. (50 sts)

Round 13: Ch 1, turn. *Sc in next ch 1 sp, ch 1, sc in next ch 1 sp, ch 1, sc2tog in next 2 ch 1 sps, ch 1; repeat from * around to last ch 1 sp. Sc in last ch 1 sp, ch 1. Join. (38 sts)

Fasten off.

HOOD SECTION

Placing the "joining seam" at the back, you will now begin working in rows, turning the work after each one.

Join the yarn to a ch-1 space at the front center of the cowl.

Row 1: Ch 1. *Sc in next ch-1 sp, ch 1; repeat from * 17 times total, sc in next ch-1 sp. (35 sts)

Row 2: Ch 1, turn. *Sc in next ch-1 sp, ch 1; repeat from * across, sc in turning ch-1 from previous row. (35 sts))

Repeat row 2 until hood measures 10–11 in./ 25.4–27.9 cm (or desired height).

Fasten off, leaving a long tail to sew hood seam.

Using a yarn needle and the long tail left from fastening off, sew the hood seam using a basic whipstitch, or a stitch of your choice.

SPIKES

Hood shown has 9 spikes. Make more or less, if you prefer.

Using Charisma and size K-10.5 crochet hook, ch 2.

Round 1: 3sc in 2nd ch from hook. Join. (3 sts)

Round 2: Ch 1. 2sc in same st, *2sc in next st; repeat from * around. Join. (6 sts)

Round 3: Ch 1. Sc in same st, 2sc in next st, *sc in next st, 2sc in next st; rep from * around. Join. (9 sts)

Round 4: Ch 1. Sc in same st, sc in next st, 2sc in next st, *sc in next 2 sts, 2sc in next st; repeat from * around. Join. (12 sts)

Round 5: Ch 1. Sc in same st, sc in next 4 sts, 2sc in next st, sc in next 5 sts, 2sc in next st. Join. (14 sts)

Rounds 6–8: Ch 1. Sc in same st, *sc in next st; repeat from * around. Join.

Fasten off, leaving a long tail to sew spike to hood.

ATTACH SPIKES

Secure each spike down the center top and back of hood using a basic tack stitch, taking each stitch in a straight up and down manner. This will help the spikes stand straight up on the hood.

TAIL

With #5 bulky weight yarn and size K-10.5 crochet hook, ch 2.

Round 1: 3sc in 2nd ch from hook. Join. (3 sts)

Round 2: Ch 1. 2sc in same st, *2sc in next st; repeat from * around. Join. (6 sts)

Round 3: Ch 1. Sc in same st, *sc in next st; repeat from * around. Join.

Fasten off, leaving a yarn tail.

Thread the yarn tail onto a yarn needle and stitch the open end closed.

Make a chain approximately 4 in./10.2 cm long, or desired length of tail.

Fasten off, leaving a long tail to sew to hood.

Using the tail at one end of the chain, secure the chain to the tail spike. Weave in ends.

Using the tail at the other end of the chain, secure tail to hood. Weave in ends.

GIRAFFE

Giraffe

This adorable giraffe hood bears a remarkable resemblance to the real thing! From the floppy ears to the cute little "horns"—this fun accessory has all the right details.

FINISHED MEASUREMENTS
Circumference: 30 in./76.2 cm
Height from top of hood to bottom edge of cowl:
  18 in./45.7 cm

YARN
Loops & Threads Zoomba (100% acrylic, 114 yd./ 104.2 m and 4.9 oz./140 g per skein), or any #6 super-bulky weight yarn

  » 3 skeins Lightning

Loops & Threads Charisma (100% acrylic, 109 yd./ 99.7 m and 3.5 oz./100 g per skein), or any #5 bulky weight yarn

  » 1 skein Off White

HOOKS AND OTHER SUPPLIES
» Size N/P-15 (10 mm) crochet hook (for hood and ears)
» Size K-10.5 (6.5 mm) crochet hook (for horns)
» Yarn needle

GAUGE

Approximately 1½ sts in dc = 1 in./2.5 cm using size N/P-15 crochet hook

Adjust hook size if necessary to obtain gauge.

Instructions

COWL SECTION

With #6 super-bulky weight yarn and size N/P-15 crochet hook, ch 44. Being careful not to twist the chain, join into a circle.

Round 1: Ch 1. Dc in same ch, *dc in next ch; repeat from * around. Join. (44 sts)

Rounds 2–5: Ch 1. Dc in same st, *dc in next st; repeat from * around. Join. (44 sts)

Round 6: Ch 1. Dc2tog, dc in each st around. Join. (43 sts)

Fasten off.

HOOD SECTION

Placing the "joining seam" at the back. You will now begin working in rows, turning the work after each one.

Count 19 stitches to the right of the back seam and attach the yarn.

Row 1: Ch 1. Dc in same st, and in next 37 sts. (38 sts)

Row 2: Ch 1, turn. Dc in same st, *dc in next st; repeat from * across. (38 sts)

Repeat row 2 until the hood section measures approximately 11–12 in./27.9–30.5 cm (or desired height).

Fasten off, leaving a long tail to sew hood seam.

Using a yarn needle and the long tail left from fastening off, sew the hood seam using a basic whipstitch, or a stitch of your choice.

EARS (MAKE 2)

With size N/P-15 crochet hook and #6 super-bulky weight yarn, ch 2.

Round 1: 10dc in 2nd chain from hook. Join. (10 sts)

Round 2: Ch 1. Dc in each st around. Join. (10 sts)

Round 3: Ch 1. *Dc in next 3 sts, dc2tog; repeat from * around. Join. (8 sts)

Round 4: Ch 1. *Dc in next 2 sts, dc2tog, dc in next 2 sts, dc2tog. Join. (6 sts)

Round 5: Ch 1. Dc in each st around. Join. (6 sts)

Fasten off, leaving a long tail to sew ear to hood.

Sew ears to hood.

HORNS (MAKE 2)

With size K-10.5 crochet hook and #5 bulky weight yarn, ch 2.

Round 1: 5sc in 2nd chain from hook. Join. (5 sts)

Round 2: Ch 1. 2sc in each st around. Join. (10 sts)

Round 3: Ch 1. Sc in each st around. Join. (10 sts)

Round 4: Ch 1. Sc in next 3 sts, sc2tog, sc in next 3 sts, sc2tog. Join. (8 sts))

Round 5: Ch 1. *Sc2tog; repeat from * around. Join. (4 sts)

Rounds 6–8: Ch 1. Sc in each st around. Join. (4 sts)

Fasten off, leaving a long tail to sew horn to hood.

Sew horns to hood.

BUNNY

Bunny

*A*dorable, floppy-eared bunnies are a favorite of many kids! The pretty beige yarn gives this hood an elegant look, and the cute long ears finish it off in perfect "bunny" detail.

FINISHED MEASUREMENTS
Circumference: 28 in./71.1 cm
Height from top of hood to bottom edge of cowl:
    19 in./48.3 cm

YARN
Loops & Threads Cozy Wool (50% wool/50% acrylic, 90 yd./82.3 m and 4.5 oz./127 g per skein), or any #6 super-bulky weight yarn

» 2 skeins Barley
» 1 skein Mushroom

HOOK AND OTHER SUPPLIES
» Size M/N-13 (9 mm) crochet hook
» Yarn needle

GAUGE
Approximately 1½ sts in dc = 1 in./2.5 cm
Adjust hook size if necessary to obtain gauge.

Instructions

COWL SECTION

With Barley, ch 42. Being careful not to twist the chain, join into a circle.

Round 1: Ch 1. Dc in same ch, *dc in next ch; repeat from * around. Join. (42 sts)

Rounds 2–7: Ch 1. Dc in same st, *dc in next st; repeat from * around. Join. (42 sts)

Fasten off.

HOOD SECTION

Placing the "joining seam" at the back, you will now begin working in rows, turning the work after each one.

Count 20 stitches to the right of the back seam and attach the yarn.

Row 1: Ch 1. Dc in same st, and in next 39 sts. (40 sts)

Row 2: Ch 1, turn. Dc in same st, *dc in next st; repeat from * across. (40 sts)

Repeat row 2 until hood measures 12–13 in./ 30.5–33 cm (or desired height).

Fasten off, leaving a long tail to sew hood seam.

Using a yarn needle and the long tail left from fastening off, sew the hood seam using a basic whipstitch or a stitch of your choice.

EARS (MAKE 2)

With Barley, ch 16.

Round 1: Dc in 3rd ch, dc in each ch across to last chain, and 2dc in last ch.

Continue working around and on the other side of the foundation chain (in the left over 3rd loops). Dc into each loop across to last chain, 2dc in last chain, join to first dc.

Round 2: Cut Barley yarn and attach Mushroom yarn to same st. Sc in each st around the ear. Join to first sc.

Fasten off, leaving a long tail to sew ears to hood.

Sew ears to hood.

FOX

Fox

If your little guy or gal has a fondness for foxes, then this cute crochet hood is just right! It features a pretty orange-colored yarn and an easy button-on style. You may even want to wear it yourself!

FINISHED MEASUREMENTS
Circumference: 32 in./81.3 cm
Height from top of hood to bottom edge of cowl:
   22 in./55.9 cm

YARN
Loops & Threads Cozy Wool (50% wool/50% acrylic, 90 yd./82.3 m and 4.5 oz./127 g per skein)

>> 3 skeins Harvest
>> 1 skein Black

HOOK AND OTHER SUPPLIES
>> Size M/N-13 (9 mm) crochet hook
>> Yarn needle
>> 3 or 4 buttons (1½ in./3.8 cm)

GAUGE
Approximately 1½–2 sts in dc = 1 in./2.5 cm
Adjust hook size if necessary to obtain gauge.

Instructions

COWL SECTION

Ch 50 with Harvest.

Row 1: Dc in 3rd ch from hook, *dc in next ch; repeat from * across. (48 sts)

Rows 2–7: Ch 1, turn. Dc in each st across.

Fasten off.

HOOD SECTION

Attach Harvest yarn to the 4th st from the edge.

Row 1: Ch 1. Dc in same st, dc in next 41 sts. (42 sts)

Row 2: Ch 1, turn. Dc in each st across.

Repeat row 2 until hood measures 12 in./30.5 cm (or desired height).

Fasten off, leaving a long tail to sew hood seam.

Using a yarn needle and the long tail left from fastening off, sew the hood seam using a basic whipstitch or a stitch of your choice.

EARS (MAKE 2)

With Harvest yarn, ch 9, leaving a long tail to sew ear to hood.

Row 1: Dc in 4th ch from hook (skipped 3 chains count as 1 dc), dc in each ch across. (7 sts)

Row 2: Ch 1, turn. Dc in first st, dc2tog, dc in next st, dc2tog, dc in last st. (5 sts)

Row 3: Ch 1, turn. Dc2tog, dc in next st, dc2tog. (3 sts)

Change to Black yarn.

Row 4: Ch 1, turn. Dc3tog.

Fasten off.

Sew ears to hood.

Attach buttons to one side of the front of the cowl section and use the space in between the stitches on the other side as buttonholes.

BEAR

Bear

Crochet this adorable bear hood for your little girl or boy! It's easy to make and incredibly cozy to wear on those chilly fall and winter days.

FINISHED MEASUREMENTS
Circumference: 32 in./81.3 cm
Height from top of hood to bottom edge of cowl: 22 in./55.9 cm

YARN
Lion Brand Yarn Wool-Ease Thick & Quick (80% acrylic/20% wool, 106 yd./96.9 m and 6 oz./170 g per skein), or any #6 super-bulky weight yarn

» 3 skeins Black

HOOK AND OTHER SUPPLIES
» Size M/N-13 (9 mm) crochet hook
» Yarn needle

GAUGE
Approximately 1½–2 sts in dc = 1 in./2.5 cm
Adjust hook size if necessary to obtain gauge.

Instructions

COWL SECTION

Ch 48. Being careful not to twist the chains, join into a circle.

Rounds 1–6: Ch 1. Dc in same st, *dc in next st; repeat from * around. Join. (48 sts)

Fasten off.

HOOD SECTION

You will now begin working in rows, turning the work after each one.

Beginning at the stitch that you fastened off on, count 22 sts to the right. Attach the yarn with a slip stitch.

Row 1: Row 1: Dc in same st, dc in next 8 sts, dc2tog, *dc in next 9 sts, dc2tog; repeat from * across until the last 4 sts. Leave the last 4 sts unworked. (40 sts))

Row 2: Ch 1, turn. Dc in each st across.

Repeat row 2 until hood measures approximately 12 in./30.5 cm (or desired height).

Fasten off, leaving a long tail to sew hood seam.

Using a yarn needle and the long tail left from fastening off, sew the hood seam using a basic whipstitch or a stitch of your choice.

EARS (MAKE 2)

Ch 2.

Row 1: 8hdc in 2nd chain from hook. (8 sts)

Row 2: Ch 1, turn. Hdc in same st, hdc in next 2 sts, 2hdc in next st, hdc in next 3 sts, 2hdc in next st. (10 sts)

Row 3: Ch 1, turn. Sc in same st, sc in next 3 sts, 2sc in next st, sc in next 4 sts, 2sc in next st. (12 sts)

Fasten off, leaving a long tail to sew ears to hood.

Sew ears to hood.

WOLF

Wolf

*Y*ou'll most likely find that this charming wolf hood isn't scary at all! It's more "cute and cuddly" than "big and bad." It makes a fun accessory for both boys and girls.

FINISHED MEASUREMENTS
Circumference: 30 in./76.2 cm
Height from top of hood to bottom edge of cowl: 15 in./38.1 cm

YARN
Loops & Threads Cozy Wool (50% wool/50% acrylic, 90 yd./82.3 m and 4.5 oz./127 g per skein), or any #6 super-bulky weight yarn

- » 2 skeins Pewter
- » 1 skein Fleece
- » 1 skein Black

Optional Hood Trim: Yarn Bee Romantique (80% acrylic/20% polyamide, 87 yd./79.6 m and 3.5 oz./100 g), or any #5 bulky weight yarn with a fuzzy texture

- » 1 skein Mist

HOOKS AND OTHER SUPPLIES
- » Size M/N-13 (9 mm) crochet hook (for cowl/hood)
- » Size L (8 mm) crochet hook (for ears)
- » Yarn needle

GAUGE

Approximately 1½–2 sts in dc = 1 in./2.5 cm, using size M/N-13 crochet hook
Adjust hook size if necessary to obtain gauge.

Instructions

COWL SECTION

With Black, ch 50.

Row 1: Dc in 3rd ch from hook (skipped chains do *not* count as a stitch), dc in each chain across. Turn. (48 sts)

Row 2: Change to Fleece. Ch 1. Hdc in each st across. Turn.

Row 3: Change to Pewter. Ch 2. Dc in each st across.

Continue with Pewter for the remainder of the cowl and hood.

Row 4: Ch 1, turn. Sc in each st across.

Row 5: Ch 2, turn. Dc in each st across.

Row 6: Ch 1, turn. Sc in each st across.

Fasten off.

HOOD SECTION

With RS of work facing, attach yarn to the 4th st from the edge (leaving 3 sts unworked).

Row 1: Ch 2. Dc in same st, dc in next 41 sts leaving last 3 sts unworked. Turn. (42 sts)

Row 2: Ch2, turn. Dc in each st across. (42 sts)

Repeat row 2 until hood measures approximately 11–12 in./27.9–30.5 cm.

Fasten off, leaving a long tail to sew hood seam.

Using a yarn needle and the long tail left from fastening off, sew the hood seam using a basic whipstitch or a stitch of your choice.

OPTIONAL HOOD EDGING

Attach #5 bulky weight fuzzy yarn to the bottom right-hand side corner stitch at the front of the hood, with a slip stitch.

Ch 1. Work sc evenly around the front opening of the hood. Fasten off.

EARS (MAKE 2)

With Pewter and size L crochet hook, ch 8, leaving a long tail to sew ear to hood.

Row 1: Dc in 2nd ch from hook and in each ch across. (7 sts)

Row 2: Ch 1, turn. Dc in first st, dc2tog, dc in next st, dc2tog, dc in last st. (5 sts)

Row 3: Ch 1, turn. Dc2tog, dc in next st, dc2tog. (3 sts)

Row 4: Ch 1, turn. Dc3tog.

Fasten off.

Using long tail from beginning edge, sew ear to hood.

Repeat for other ear.

ATTACH BUTTONS

Attach 2 buttons to one side of the front of the cowl section. Button the cowl closed by slipping the buttons through the stitches on the other side of the cowl.

Crochet Stitch Refresher

Slipknot

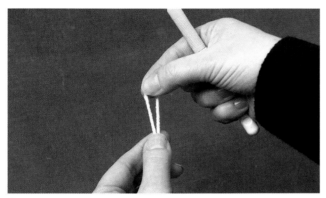

1. Fold the end of the yarn to form a loop.

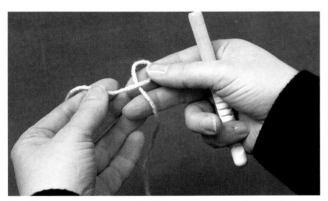

2. Cross the loose end of the yarn over the end that is attached to the ball of yarn.

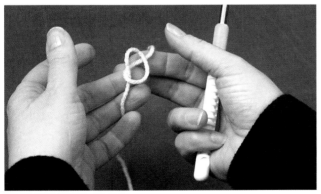

3. Continue to bring the loose end of the yarn behind the loop.

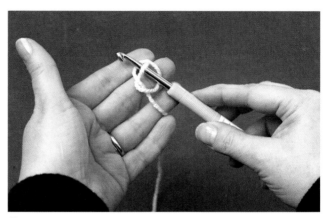

4. Insert the crochet hook underneath, and out the other side, of the piece of yarn that is behind the loop.

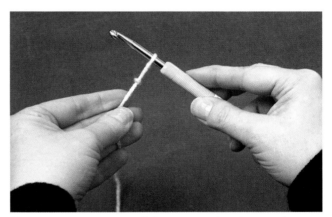

5. Pull the two ends of the yarn tight, closing the knotted loop around the crochet hook. Slipknot is made and attached to hook.

Beginning Chain

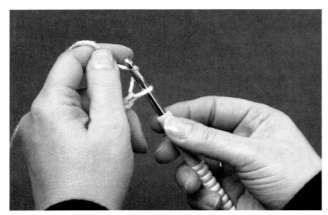

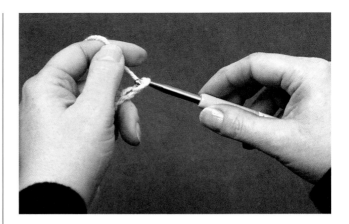

1. Begin by making a slipknot on the crochet hook and bring the yarn from back to front over the hook.

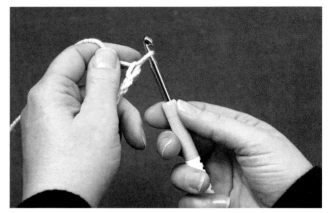

2. Pull yarn through the loop on the hook. Chain stitch completed.

3. Continue bringing the yarn from front to back over the hook and pulling it through the loop on the hook until you have the desired number of chain stitches.

Single Crochet

1. Insert hook into next stitch.

2. Yarn over hook.

3. Bring the hook through the stitch and pull up a loop.

4. Yarn over hook.

5. Pull through both loops on hook.

Single Crochet Decrease (sc2tog)

Insert hook in next stitch, yarn over and pull up loop (2 loops on hook), insert hook in next stitch, yarn over and pull up loop (3 loops on hook), yarn over and draw through all 3 loops on hook.

Half Double Crochet

1. Yarn over hook.

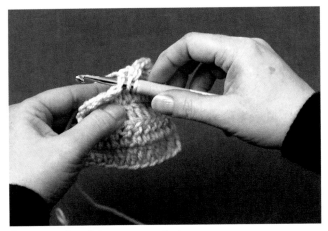

2. Insert hook into next stitch.

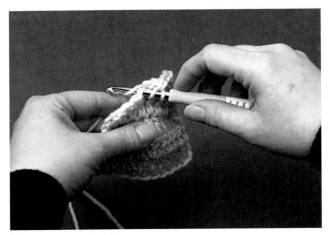

3. Yarn over hook.

4. Bring the hook through the stitch and pull up a loop.

5. Yarn over hook.

6. Pull through three loops on hook.

Half Double Crochet Decrease (hdc2tog)

[Yarn over, insert hook in next stitch, yarn over and pull up loop] 2 times, yarn over and draw through all loops on hook.

Double Crochet

1. Yarn over hook.

2. Insert hook into next stitch.

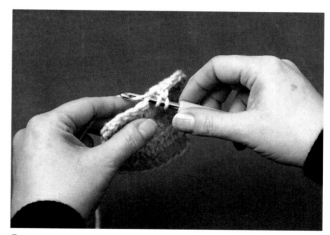

3. Yarn over hook.

4. Bring the hook through the stitch and pull up a loop.

5. Yarn over hook.

6. Pull through two loops on hook.

7. Yarn over hook.

8. Pull through two loops on hook.

Double Crochet Decrease (dc2tog)

[Yarn over, insert hook in next stitch, yarn over and pull up loop, yarn over, draw through 2 loops] 2 times, yarn over, draw through all loops on hook.

Double Crochet Double Decrease (dc3tog)

[Yarn over, insert hook into next stitch, yarn over and pull up a loop, yarn over, draw through 2 loops] 3 times, yarn over, draw through all loops on hook.

Treble Crochet

1. Yarn over hook twice.

2. Insert hook into next stitch.

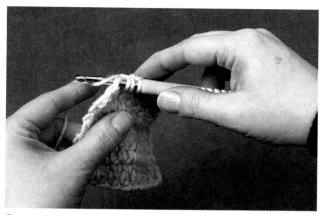

3. Yarn over hook.

4. Bring the hook through the stitch and pull up a loop.

5. Yarn over hook.

6. Pull through two loops on hook.

7. Yarn over hook.

8. Pull through two loops on hook.

9. Yarn over hook.

10. Pull through two loops on hook.

Working into Front Loop or Back Loop Only

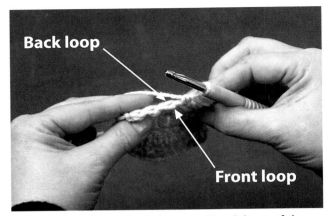

Back loop

Front loop

Arrows point to the front loop and back loop of the stitch.

Front loop only: Insert hook into the *front loop only* of the stitch, leaving the back loop unworked. Work stitch as normal.

Back loop only: Insert hook into the *back loop only* of the stitch, leaving the front loop unworked. Work stitch as normal.

Post Stitches

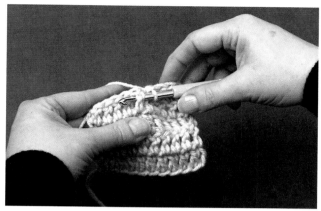

To work a front post stitch, work the stitch that you're about to make as normal except, instead of working into the loops at the top of the stitch, **insert the hook behind the next stitch on the row below** *and back to the front of the work.*

FRONT POST DOUBLE CROCHET (FPDC)

Yarn over, insert hook from front to back to front around post of corresponding stitch below, yarn over and pull up loop [yarn over, draw through 2 loops on hook] 2 times.

FRONT POST TREBLE CROCHET (FPTR)

Yarn over twice, insert hook from front to back to front around post of corresponding stitch below, yarn over and pull up loop [yarn over, draw through 2 loops on hook] 3 times.

BACK POST DOUBLE CROCHET (BPDC)

Yarn over, insert hook from *back to front to back* around post of corresponding stitch below, yarn over and pull up loop [yarn over, draw through 2 loops on hook] 2 times.

Abbreviations

2dc	work 2 double crochet stitches into same stitch
2sc	work 2 single crochet stitches into same stitch
BLO	back loop only
bpdc	back post double crochet
ch	chain
dc	double crochet
dc2tog	double crochet 2 together
dc3tog	double crochet 3 together
fpdc	front post double crochet
fptr	front post treble crochet
hdc	half double crochet
hdc2tog	half double crochet 2 stitches together
RS	right side
sc	single crochet
sc2tog	single crochet 2 stitches together
sk	skip
sl	slip
sp	space
st/sts	stitch/stitches
tr	treble crochet
WS	wrong side
yo	yarn over

Yarn Sources

The following are the sources of the yarns used in the samples in this book, but many yarns are available that would make excellent substitutions. To substitute, find a yarn of the same weight and similar fiber content, and always check your gauge!

Lion Brand Yarn
lionbrand.com
Available in most craft stores.

Loops & Threads
michaels.com
Available exclusively through Michaels.

I Love This Yarn!
hobbylobby.com
Available exclusively through Hobby Lobby.

Acknowledgments

Thank you to Tanya Haswell for her wonderful photography.

Thank you to Stackpole Books for working with me and allowing me the opportunity to put this book together.

Visual Index

Adult Hoods, Cowls, and Scarves

Cluster Stitch Hood   3

Slanted Shells Snood   6

Cozy Cable Hood   9

Knit-Look Snood   12

Linen Stitch Hood   16

Puff Stitch Snood   20

Herringbone Hooded Scarf   23

Chunky Ribbed Hood   27

Faux Cable Snood   31

Animal Hoods

Kitty Cat 77

Dinosaur 81

Giraffe 85

Bunny 88

Fox 91

Bear 95

Wolf 99